Peeps® BRAND

Cross-Stitch Book

INSTRUCTIONS AND PATTERNS

Text and patterns by
Sosae and Dennis Caetano

RP MINIS
PHILADELPHIA

RP Minis®
Hachette Book Group
1290 Avenue of the Americas, New York, NY 10104
www.runningpress.com
@Running_Press

First Edition: January 2026

Published by RP Minis, an imprint of Hachette Book Group, Inc. The RP Minis name and logo is a registered trademark of Hachette Book Group, Inc.

Contact specialmarkets@hbgusa.com regarding special discounts for bulk purchases.

Design by Tanvi Baghele

ISBN: 978-0-7624-8842-1

Made in Dongguan, China (HKD) 09/25 #01

Introduction

Welcome to the sweet and squishy worl of PEEPS®! If your PEEPSONALITY leans toward marshmallow and cross stitch, you've come to the right place Here you'll find everything you need t stitch four perfectly Peeptastic designs Party Peeps; Two Peeps Are Better Tha One; Live, Laugh, Peeps; and Peeps I My Superpower.

Included in this kit are threads in pink, ye low, green, orange, blue, purple, and brow Also included are two tapestry needle three sheets of aida fabric, a beautiful dis

Contents

lay hoop, and, of course, this mini instruc-
ion and pattern book.

If you're new to cross-stitch, read this
ook for a complete introduction on how to
hread your needle and how to make those
retty little *x*-stitches. For more experi-
nced stitchers, you can jump right to the
atterns on page 23.

As you probably know by now, PEEPS®
ren't just for eating, although we do enjoy
hat too. They also make cute and quirky
nasterpieces and are the perfect way to
xpress your creativity. So grab your sup-
lies, get comfy, and stitch yourself (or a
iend) an adorable Peepsake.

Cross-Stitch Basics

Cross-stitch style is a particular style o embroidery, one in which you'll use relatively blunt needle—called a tapestr needle—to sew *x*-shaped stitches onto you fabric surface, creating a picture (in ou case, of super adorable PEEPS®). Here ar a few basics to get you started!

Supplies

One of the benefits of cross-stitch is ho easy it is to get started—you'll only nee a few tools to begin working. With cross stitch fabric, tapestry needles, embroider floss, a hoop, and some sharp scissors, you'll be whipping up PEEPS® keepsakes in no time.

FABRIC

Aida cloth is made specifically for cross-stitch projects. It is comprised of tiny squares so it is easy to see where each stitch in your pattern belongs. There are three pieces of aida cloth included in this kit to get you started! If you're in need of more aida, don't fret: It's easy to find at your local craft store or online.

NEEDLES

For any kind of embroidery project, you'l need a needle to pull your thread throug the fabric. With cross-stitch, the best tool i a tapestry needle—the relatively dull poin on these needles will go through your fabri without snagging or tearing. There are tw needles included in this kit—you only nee one while you work, but it doesn't hurt t have an extra on hand.

THREAD

Thread is the most important, and the mos fun, part of your cross-stitch toolkit. All o the patterns in this book use embroider floss, which is a type of six-stranded thread that is especially well-suited to cross-stitch. (When you stitch, you will only use two strands at once. More on that later!) We've included seven skeins of thread that correspond with the patterns in this book.

HOOP

Included in this kit is a 3-inch plastic hoop; all four patterns in this kit are designed to fit within it. A hoop is a wonderful way to display your finished cross-stitch project. Simply trim the excess aida, or tape it behind the hoop, and your masterpiece is ready for display or gifting.

SCISSORS

A pair of regular scissors will do in a pinch, but an extra-sharp pair will come in handy if you need to remove any stitches or get into small areas. Always be careful when using your embroidery scissors.

Let's Get Stitchin'

Before you begin stitching your Peeptacular masterpiece, you'll need to get your fabric ready. Though it's not necessary, we recommend a gentle run of the iron over your aida pieces, as they may have folds from packaging. Once it's crisp and flat, it's easy to hold and begin stitching. Aida is a sturdy fabric, and stitching without a hoop is quite easy and versatile. (The added bonus is that you don't get any hoop creases!) But if you choose to stitch with a hoop, here's how: Unscrew the tightening device at the top of the hoop until it's loose enough to remove the inner ring. Place your aida on top of the inner ring so that the ring is centered under the aida. Then, place the outer hoop over the aida and the inner hoop so that you are sandwiching the aida between the two hoops. Press down so the outer ring covers the inner ring completely, then tighten the screw at the top of the outer hoop so that the fabric is taut.

Next, thread your needle. Find the color that corresponds to the stitches that are in the center of your pattern (more on that in a moment) and cut a piece of thread that is roughly 18 inches long. You'll then want to separate your piece of thread into strands. (Each piece of embroidery thread is made up of six distinct strands, though you'll only want to use two at a time when stitching.) Gently pull two strands away from the remaining four, being careful not to tangle them. Once apart, put the remaining four strands aside for use later. Snip the ends of the two strands you'll be working with to give you a crisp edge for threading the needle. Feed the strands into the eye of the needle, leaving a short "tail" on one side (4 inches is good). Don't knot the thread!

MAKING CROSS-STITCHES

Your stitches will move from the center of the pattern outward. The patterns in this book use a method called "counted cross-stitch," meaning that you will base your stitches on a pattern rather than a design printed on the fabric. With this type of pattern, you'll count the number of stitches in the color you're using and then make those stitches on your fabric. So, to get started, find the center of your fabric—you don't need to be super precise, but try to get as close to the center as possible. This is where you'll want to begin stitching.

Once you've found the center of your fabric, you can begin making stitches.

1. To start, pull your thread up through the small hole at the **bottom left** corner of your starting square, being sure to leave a 1-inch "tail" of floss on the underside of the fabric. Hold on to that tail as you make your next few stitches right on top of it—you'll want the back side of your stitches to cover the tail, securing it in place.

2. Pull the thread up through the fabric and then sew through the **top right** corner of the same square, creating a diagonal stitch. Pull your thread through to the back of the fabric, taking care not to pull it too tightly—your goal should be a smooth surface, without any puckering from the floss. This is the first half of your stitch.
3. To create the second half of your stitch, sew up from the back of the fabric—through the **bottom right** corner of the square—to the front.

4. Pull your thread relatively taut, and then cross the square diagonally, sewing down through the **top left** hole. This will create the *x* shape of your cross-stitch.

5. Continue by making a stitch in the **bottom left** corner of the square next to your completed stitch. This square borders your first stitch and shares two holes with it.

MAKING A ROW OF CROSS-STITCHES

To work a row in the same color, create the first half of each of the stitches by repeating steps 2 and 3 from the previous list, moving from left to right until you've created a row of diagonal half-stitches all going from bottom left to top right.

When you reach the end of the row, bring your needle up through the bottom right hole and work your way back across, completing the *x* shape of each square as you go.

BACKSTITCHING

To stitch the fine outlines in each pattern, you will use a technique called backstitch. (Backstitching is done once all the cross-stitching is complete.) To begin, thread your needle with two strands of the designated color floss and weave it into a few stitches on the back of your work. This will secure it.

Following the pattern for placement, bring the needle up to the surface and make a stitch over (or across, depending on the pattern) one square of aida. To make the next stitch, come up one square away from the previous stitch and go back down into the previous stitch. (Hence, *back*stitch!) It's okay and sometimes necessary to "break" an aida square when backstitching. That means you bring your needle through in the middle of a square, or off to one side, instead of through the premade holes in the aida. Just follow the pattern as best you can and have fun with it. Your cross-stitch will look great.

MAKING A FRENCH KNOT

To stitch the eyes and nose (and the centers of the little orange flowers), you will use an embroidery stitch called a French knot. To make a French knot, weave the thread into a few stitches in the back of the work to secure it, then bring it up to the surface of the design where the knot will be. (Note: It's necessary to use both hands in the process of making a French knot, so place your aida down on your lap or a table for the next part.)

With one hand, hold the thread upward and make it taut. Wrap the thread around the needle twice, still holding it taut so it doesn't slip off the needle. Then insert the needle back into the aida a tiny bit away from where it came out, pulling all the way down until the thread tightens itself into a neat little knot on the surface of the aida. This technique is simple and quick, but it takes practice. Feel free to try it a few times on test fabric first. You'll get the hang of it in no time!

Tip: When you're done with one French knot, move right along to the next without cutting the thread. Weave in the end when all French knots of the same color are complete.

HELPFUL TIPS

- For a polished look, make all your stitches in the same direction and order: from the bottom left to the top right, and then the bottom right to the top left.
- To display your work, soak it in a warm bath to remove any hoop creases. Let it dry flat. (Do not wring.)

Patterns

Party Peeps

Thread Colors

PINK YELLOW BLUE

PURPLE BROWN

Two Peeps Are Better Than One

Thread Colors

PINK YELLOW GREEN ORANGE

PURPLE BROWN

Live, Laugh, Peeps

Thread Colors

PINK YELLOW GREEN

PURPLE BROWN

Peeps Is My Superpower

Thread Colors

PINK YELLOW ORANGE

BLUE BROWN